CHRISTIAN OCCASIONS

CHRISTIAN OCCASIONS

Photographs and Text
by Alan Whitman

A **COUNTRY MUSIC** Magazine Press Book
Dolphin Books
Doubleday & Company, Inc. Garden City, New York
1978

1-24-79

A Country Music Magazine Press Book

ISBN: 0-385-12597-6
Library of Congress Catalog Card Number 77-76286
Copyright ©1978 by KBO Publishers, Inc.
All Rights Reserved
Printed in the United States of America
First Edition

Editor: Jim Menick
Designer: Cheh Nam Low

To Patrick Carr

ACKNOWLEDGMENTS

To the many people who helped with this book, I express my appreciation.

In particular, Gayle Sheard, Peggy Greene, Bill Henry, Xiomara Whitman, Torrey Whitman and my parents sustained me and endured me while I worked on the project. Liz Huntington, Nancy Fleming, Charlotte Legg, John Murray and Gary Mohon helped me track down some of the events. Tom and Marguerite Hays helped make time and money available for me to go and do the work. Jim Pitts provided insight and understanding when things seemed incomprehensible.

And thanks especially to Jim Menick and Nels Johnson at Doubleday, and to Cheh Nam Low at *Country Music* magazine for assistance and support in the production of the book, and to Patrick Carr for editorial guidance and direction.

INTRODUCTION

In July of 1976, Patrick Carr, then editor of *Country Music* Magazine Press, called to ask if I'd be interested in doing a book about grassroots American Christianity. He had in mind a series of photo essays on out-of-the-ordinary religious activities and unusual services.

I was right in the middle of the Bible Belt and I found things I knew of but had never paid much attention to: faith healers, fundamentalist evangelists, tent revivals, drive-in churches, lakeside services, all-night gospel sings—many almost in my own backyard in Greenville, South Carolina—things I had passed by on the road, or had seen advertised on auditorium marquees or in newspapers, or had heard about from friends. Our working title was *Christian Occasions,* which limited the scope of the book to public services and celebrations through which the Word is taken to the people rather than the more structured congregational church services with their fixed memberships.

Since I was not a Christian I did not relate to what I saw as a believer—I did not know what it felt like to believe that Jesus Christ is Lord. I watched and listened, and responded with my camera. I was among people whom I knew, had grown up with and considered as my friends. They accepted me into their midst during intensely personal moments in their lives, and made me feel welcome, and I was honest and straightforward with them.

I have tried to keep as much of the participants' own words as possible, which is why most of the text which follows is in quotation marks. Except in one or two obvious places, all the text prefaced by a dash is my own.

I was often amazed at what I saw, and sometimes I did not understand what happened, but I know it did happen. This book is my response to those happenings.

CHRISTIAN OCCASIONS

I will give thanks to the Lord with my whole heart;
I will tell of all thy wonderful deeds.
I will be glad and exult in thee,
I will sing praise to thy name, O, Most High.
                                    —Psalm 9

Getting Saved

"The day came that LaVerne was awarded the part as lead singer with The Blue Ridge Quartet. Before this he had sung with two different groups. He worked at various jobs to support us, and many times we were sure we'd starve, but our beautiful Lord had His hand on LaVerne, and took care of the three of us. Life, at times, was hard. Money was scarce, and we dreamed of the day when someone would recognize his talent. However, it didn't come when we wanted it to. As we look back now, we can easily see the L-O-N-G Suffering Savior taking care of a young, determined, foolish boy that would one day be involved in a nation-wide Soul-Winning ministry. We cannot begin to explain why God chose him, but we are positive that God has many greater areas yet for us to enter. For many months, LaVerne has felt God leading him into a healing ministry, yet he feels that his strongest area is being a Soul Winner. Only a few services so far, has he called for the sick to come forward. Yet, God has given many, almost unbelievable miracles as he prayed. This is an area in which we sincerely need your prayerful support!! Please Pray!"

—Edith Tripp in LIFE STORY OF EDITH & LAVERNE

LaVerne Tripp is an evangelist of the Pentecostal Holiness Church, which believes in the fiery baptism by the Holy Spirit. Speaking in tongues is widespread, and the services are "joyous demonstrations."

Tripp is a gospel singer—he was once a member of the highly successful Blue Ridge Quartet—and he calls his ministry The LaVerne Tripp Song Revival. He received his calling to evangelism in 1975, and, after failing to persuade the other members of the Blue Ridge Quartet to accompany him on the evangelical path, left the group to form his ministry.

Tripp travels over three hundred days a year, mainly in the South and Northeast, and has syndicated radio and television shows. Although the Pentecostal Holiness Church believes in divine healing, the song revival is primarily a soul-winning crusade.

"I want to tell you something tonight. Jesus Christ is coming. The Word of God plainly tells us. We see certain things happening; we see certain signs on this earth and certain signs in the heavens. All of these signs and all of those things that Jesus said would be happening when the coming of the Lord would be at the door are taking place tonight. And what I'm going to share with you tonight, it'll blow your mind.

"I'm going to tell you what the scientists and astronomers and astrologers are saying, and then I'm going to show you what the Word of God says. The scientists have discovered that the nine planets in our solar system are lining up. Now, they have been in perfect alignment before . . . have you heard a story about one night some shepherds were on a hillside, and they looked into the heavens and saw a bright star shining? Have you heard that story before? The planets, according to history, were in perfect alignment at that time. And they're fixing to line up again.

"Before I tell you what is going to happen, let me tell you what the scientists said. They said that when the planets line up it's gonna cause the worst earthquakes this world has ever known since the beginning of history. The sun is going to get so hot and so bright that it's gonna burn up almost all of its energy and go almost completely out, and this earth will be placed in almost total darkness.

"Now let me tell you what the Word of God says, and if you don't believe me, when you get home read the sixteenth chapter of the Book of Revelations, the last book in the Bible. The Bible tells us that at the end of the time of tribulation, the fourth angel out of the last seven pours his bile on the sun, and the sun gets so hot that it scorches and burns men's bodies and they curse and blaspheme God because of it. God's Word tells us that the fifth angel pours his bile on the king of beasts, which is the antichrist and his kingdom is this earth, and the Bible says his kingdom is placed into darkness. It sounds as if the scientists took the Word of God and copied verbatim the things that are gonna happen when the planets align.

"According to the scientists, the planets are going to line up in December of 1982."

—What do you feel when you see that—knowing that the real thing is there and that you were the one who enabled people to reach it tonight?

"I get caught in the real movement, you know. I realize that I am sent—I am sent of God. So I have a mission. I have a responsibility relative to God. Not to them, the people, but to God. And that's a heavy responsibility. They have a responsibility to Him too, but the responsibilities are different."

—A couple of girls really seemed to be having deep emotional experiences. What did they go through?

"Most people that you see do that, they do it for two reasons. One is for show—to get attention—and one is, you're genuine, it's really real. Those two tonight, that boy and that girl, during the whole service—and I'm not condemning and I'm not a judge—I feel like they were doing it for attention. But there were several others at different times during the service, the real thing was there."

Miracle On The Mountain

"There it stands as immovable as the mountain in a location chosen by the Providence of God. People will be coming to look upon this Portrayal a thousand years from now if the Lord permits this world to exist that long."

—Gerald L.K. Smith in THE MIRACLE ON THE MOUNTAINS

—The miracles here are found on Magnetic Mountain, just outside Eureka Springs, in the Ozark mountains of northwestern Arkansas. They are the creation of Gerald L.K. Smith, proclaimed in his park literature as "this century's greatest defender of Christianity and Americanism."

The giant statue of Christ, called "Christ of the Ozarks," is the work of Emmet Sullivan, "world renowned as the sculptor of the largest group of Dinosaurs in the world." The statue stands seven stories high, has an armspread from fingertip to fingertip of sixty five feet and weighs something over one million pounds.

The amphitheater in which the Great Passion Play is presented is located on Mount Oberammergau. The animals used in the play are imported from the Middle East; the cast consists of about a hundred local residents. Writer-producer-director Robert Hyde plays the part of Jesus.

Construction is underway, but far from completed, on the New Holy Land, a twenty million dollar project which will feature shrines of places visited by Jesus while He was on earth. At each shrine actors will portray the events as recorded in the New Testament.

In 1973, Gerald L.K. Smith wrote: "We do not need to travel around the world, because the world comes to us at Eureka Springs." Smith died in April, 1976. He is buried near the base of the statue.

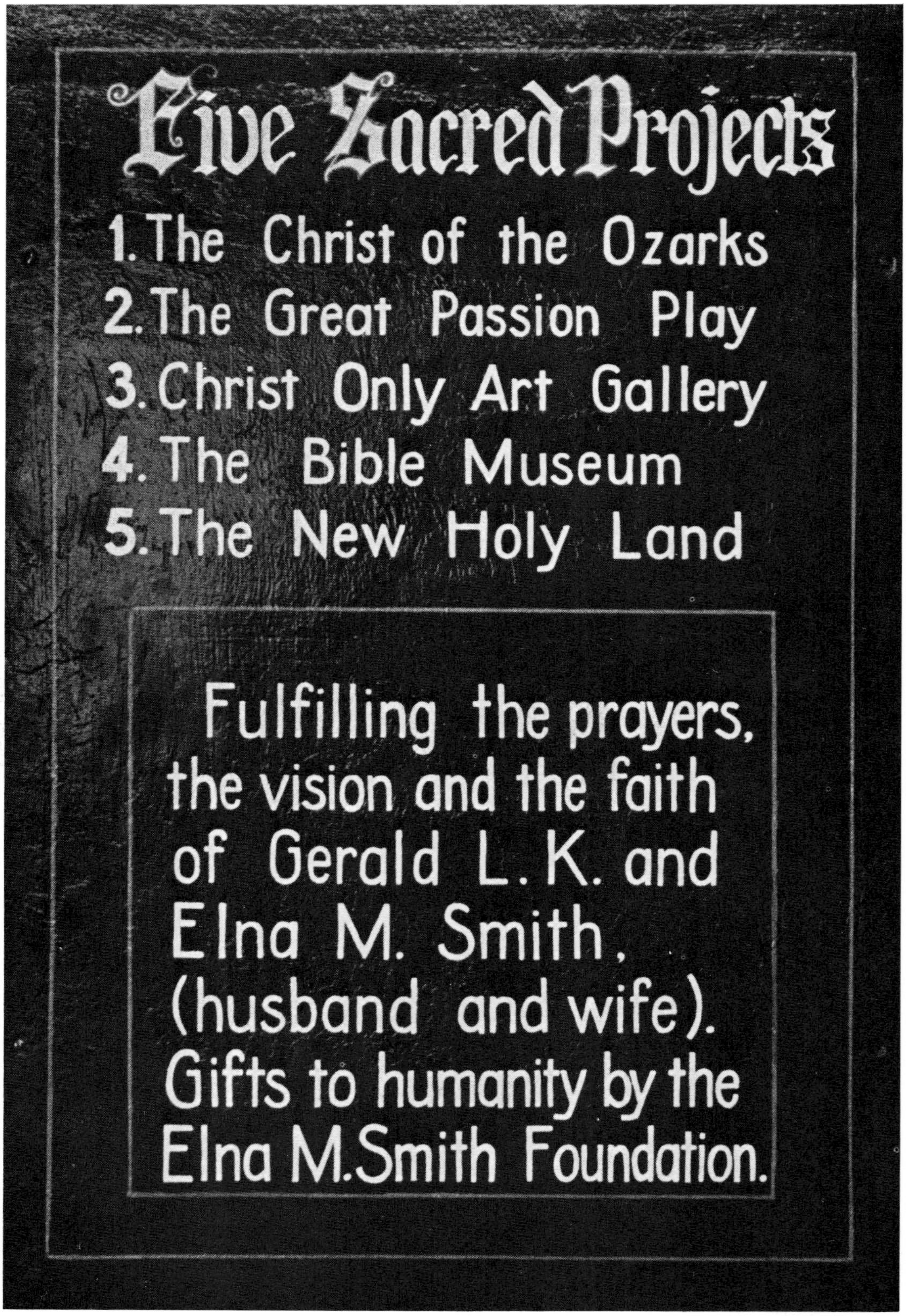

Five Sacred Projects

1. The Christ of the Ozarks
2. The Great Passion Play
3. Christ Only Art Gallery
4. The Bible Museum
5. The New Holy Land

Fulfilling the prayers, the vision and the faith of Gerald L. K. and Elna M. Smith, (husband and wife). Gifts to humanity by the Elna M. Smith Foundation.

THE GREAT PASSION PLAY

"The severest critics now pronounce it as the greatest presentation of our Lord's last week in Christian history. Journalists and students of ecclesiastical drama have journeyed all the way from every free nation on earth and all the states to see this presentation."

—MIRACLE ON THE MOUNTAIN brochure

20

"This is the story of a man—a man born into a society crying from the pain of despair, fear, and oppression, a man born in a land of desolation, hunger, and doom—the man destined to be the long awaited Messiah. This is the story of Jesus of Nazareth and the greatest event in the history of Christian mankind, the DIVINE TRAGEDY."

—from the Prologue, THE GREAT PASSION PLAY

"One night in Hollywood, California, I awoke at 3 o'clock and reflected on what might happen in case war demolished or further marred the original Holy Land. Out of this concern came an inspired vision, and I announced to the world that we were going to rebuild the Holy Land as it was when Jesus was on earth. This construction is now in process. It will require several years to complete, and will cost approximately $20,000,000.00 or more.

"At each shrine will be actors who will portray for the visitors the events as recorded in the New Testament whether it be the Sermon on the Mount, or Jesus visiting with the woman at the well."

—Gerald L.K. Smith in AN OPEN LETTER FROM GERALD L.K. SMITH

THESE ARE ENGINEERING MODELS OF THE BUILDINGS
TO BE CONSTRUCTED IN THE NEW HOLY LAND APPROXIMAT-
ELY ½ MILE EAST OF THIS SITE. THE ACTUAL BUILDINGS
WILL BE LIFE-SIZE; BY COMPARISON, A MAN, IN THE SCALE
OF THESE MODELS WOULD BE .5½ INCHES TALL.
    THE CONSTRUCTION OF THIS AWE-INSPIRING PROJECT IS
NOW UNDERWAY AND WILL BE OPENED TO THE PUBLIC, IN
ITS VARIOUS STAGES AS THEY ARE DEVELOPED. NEW
PHASES WILL BE ADDED EACH YEAR UNTIL THE ENTIRE
NEW HOLY LAND PROJECT IS COMPLETED. IN ADDITION
TO BUILDING THE STRUCTURES EXTANT IN CHRIST'S TIME,
THERE WILL BE PRESENTED, IN THEATRE FORM, THE MAJ-
OR EVENTS OF HIS LIFE AND MINISTRY.
    THE REPLICA OF "THE GOLDEN GATE", TO YOUR RIGHT,
WILL BE THE ENTRANCE TO THIS PROJECT, AND WILL
MEMORIALIZE THE INDIVIDUALS AND FAMILIES WHO
ARE ASSISTING FINANCIALLY IN THE CONSTRUCTION
OF THE NEW HOLY LAND.

PLEASE! DO NOT TOUCH THE MODELS

The shrines which will be reproduced in the New Holy Land in life size will include the following:
1. Temple
2. Market Streets.
3. Herod's Palace
4. House of Annas
5. Upper Room (Last Supper)
6. Bethlehem
7. House of Caiaphas
8. Pool of Siloam
9. Old City of David
10. Fortress Antonia
11. Bethany across Jordan
12. Magdala
13. Miracle of loaves and fishes
14. Bethsaida
15. Capernaum
16. Sermon on the Mount
17. Roman Theatre
18. Nazareth
19. Mount Tabor (Transfiguration)
20. Golgotha and Tomb of Christ
21. Garden of Gethsemane
22. Bethany (Tomb of Lazarus)
23. Ascension and Pater Noster
24. Palm Sunday Road
25. Sea of Galilee and River Jordan

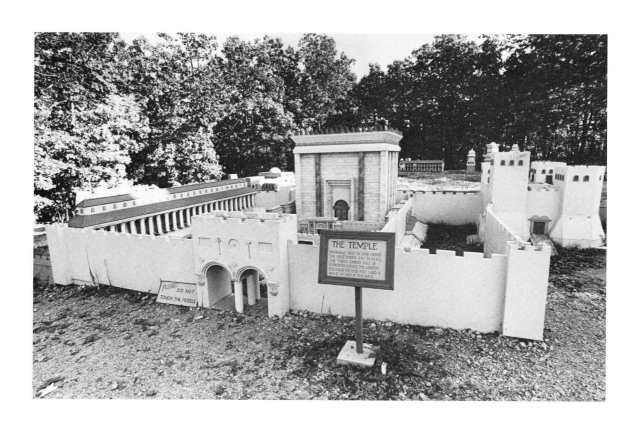

THE TEMPLE

ORIGINALLY BUILT BY KING HEROD
THE GREAT DURING 19 B.C. TO 64 A.D.
THE TEMPLE COMPLEX WILL BE
REPRESENTED EXPRESS. THE LARGEST
BUILDING IN THE HOLY LAND A
MAXIE 3/4" HIGH IN THIS SCALE

PLEASE! DO NOT TOUCH THE MODELS

From Place To Place

"I'm gonna say this tonight. I never knew too much about what persecution in the church was, but I was down in the state of Kentucky at some of these places to preach. There were several nights I thought I was going to take a whipping before I got out. Amen.

"One night I was off by myself. My wife had gone back home to put the children in school. I was there at a tent revival. Conviction was there, and it was so strong, but these people just couldn't respond. I felt because conviction was there so great that I should stay another night. So that night I announced it.

"And you know that just as soon as the benediction was said at the closing of that service, it would have been no more real to me than if a hearse had backed up there and brought a coffin in with a dead person in it. That's the spirit that fell over the tent that night. Nobody there but me. And I didn't understand it.

"I didn't have a trailer at the time and I was sleeping in the back end of the truck. That night, men came to the truck. And I woke up. I thought, Lord, there's going to be a funeral, but I didn't know it was gonna be mine.

"You say, 'Were you scared?' Honey, I was scared stiff. I believe that's why God said to spend the night there, too. I don't think it's good for one minister to ever be out alone by himself.

"I said, God, as far as my part's concerned, Lord, I don't care. But I began to think, we have nine children, all of them little. And I said, Lord, I'd rather live and raise my children till they get grown. Maybe I just might switch my living; I don't know.

"But you know, I prayed. It was raining out there. And it seemed like all of a sudden God began to let the rain really go—and He turned water buckets over on them.

"I went to sleep, and the next morning, across the road, there were a bunch of beer bottles and things like that.

"He said all that live in glory in Christ Jesus shall suffer persecution. He said if you suffer with Me, you're gonna reign with Me. But you've got to be willing to suffer."

—Brother Garrett

32

—I found the Garrett's revival tent in Greenville, South Carolina, just a few miles from my own home. On a warm August afternoon, Reverend Garrett and I sat in the tent and talked. Mrs. Garrett, who shares the services with her husband, was "keeping house" in their 23-foot trailer parked nearby. The five Garrett children who travel with their parents, and sing and play music during the service, were sweeping and straightening up the platform and the altar.

"Jesus said go out on the highways and in the hedges and compel them to come in," Reverend Garrett told me. "We feel like that's the part of the Bible we're fulfilling: we're opening the door for 'whosoever will, let him come.' People come in here who would never come into a church. They feel more freedom; they're more comfortable in a tent.

"When you have a tent ministry, you're not governed by anyone—just by God. We have more religious freedom. If we come into a church, we can only reach those that are members of that particular church, whereas here we've got a chance of reaching people of various faiths. We don't believe there's any one particular organization or one particular church.

"We have both a healing and a salvation ministry. We don't separate them: we preach them together. Our message is a warning message—it's a message of mercy and salvation. It's an opportunity. We come to a town, and we may not see a lot of conversions, but we feel that God let the tent come here; it's an opportunity that these people could have found Christ. And on the last day of Judgment, they can't say, 'You didn't send an evangelist, You didn't send the Gospel to our town.'"

The Garretts live in Ohio, and work mostly in that region—Ohio, Virginia, West Virginia, Kentucky. Greenville is the furthest they've traveled with the tent.

"We just thought to come here. We came into town, found a lot and rented it. We put announcements in the paper, and put some radio advertising on. My wife and daughter phone pastors at local churches to let them know we're here, but sometimes we don't get much cooperation from them. Some pastors seem to have the attitude that they'd rather see an evangelist not come to town, not ever see the people saved, if it isn't through their own church. We feel that people who are converted or saved in our meetings need to be established in a church and have a good pastor take them in and care for them. It makes it hard for us if the local pastors don't come out and cooperate. But we feel that once we get someone saved, and get them in Christ, that God is able to direct them to a place and keep them. If I saved them, if it was my doing, it would be up to me to keep them. But I don't do it—it's the Lord that does the saving.

"It's not an easy ministry. It's expensive to move across the country. And it's all manual labor in putting the tent up. We roll the tent out, set the stakes, and lace it up. Once the tent is up in the air, we've got to set up the platform and the lights, and dig a ditch around the tent to drain the water out. I like to have two or three days to get everything set up before we start our revival. When you go to take it down, you've got a claim to some people who will come out and help. But when you go into a community, what help you've got with you is all you've got.

"We feel our work has it's rewards—not too much in the financial end of it, although the Lord has given us enough money to go from place to place. But we see people helped that never felt the presence of God, and have never really known the reality of God. When we see them come and find Christ—well, it's rewarding."

"I don't know what it's going to take to save Greenville. I know that my Mighty God, if He has to move heaven and earth, He'll have to do it.

"I'm saying on this Saturday night, and God knows the very hour and the very day that we prayed for it. I'm saying, God, please save Greenville. I'm saying, God, save Greenville. I don't know what it's going to take, but You save it.

"Now will you come and stand in the tent with me? Around the altar right now. And I want you to ask for Greenville with me. I don't know if the revival's going on tomorrow night. God hasn't spoken yet. I just say, God, You tell me when. I'm not going to leave this area till God says it's time to go. Because there are souls to save.

"Won't you come and stand with us as we pray?

"Oh Mighty Jesus, Greenville may not see the face of God tonight. They might not. They might feel like they've got it all under control—no time for God. But I'm going to say that tomorrow they may wish that they found the time.

"Oh Mighty Jesus. If you've got confidence in yourself praying before God I want you to earnestly ask God for Greenville tonight. You might say, well, it never will happen to you. Let me tell you, it has happened before. It can happen now.

"Oh Mighty Jesus. I want every hand raised, and when you pray I want you to pray with all the confidence in God that God is going to answer your prayers. I want you to ask God for your neighbors, for your friends, for your loved ones, for your children and your children's children tonight. Because if God don't spare them, what are they going to do?

"Everyone that I don't see in on this prayer, I want you to come and stand with us tonight. It may be your prayin' that, if you ask, will fill in the gap for God to save them.

"You got prayers that are goin' up before God as a memorial. I want to hear you say, God, You save 'em no matter what the cost is. And Father, as we as individuals speak unto You tonight, Father, we have asked You for Greenville, for the loved ones in this area. We've asked You for the neighbors and the friends of these that are standing tonight.

"And we're asking You, Lord, to save them no matter what the cost may be, in Jesus' Mighty Name. In the Name of Jesus, won't You spare Greenville and save us, no matter what the cost? Save the loved ones, save the neighbors, save the friends.

"God, meet the needs of the people tonight.

"In the name of Mighty Jesus, God, as we come to You in supplication, come in. We're asking You, oh Mighty God, to move within the hearts of Greenville.

"Meet the needs, meet the needs. How we pray. How we honor You tonight. We love You, Jesus. Oh how we worship You and we praise You.

"We love You."

—Sister Garrett

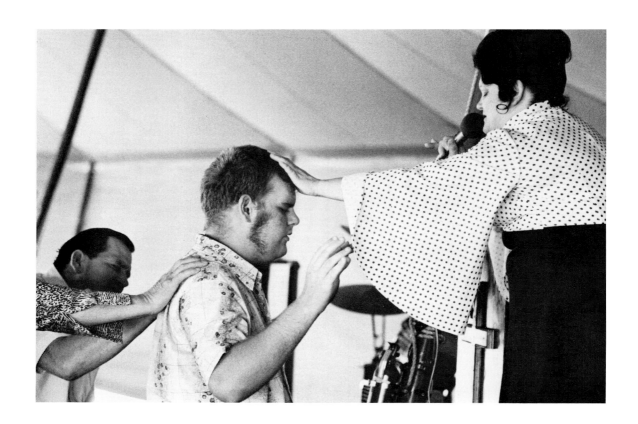

"I want you to ask Jesus to come into your life today. And I want you to talk to Him just like you would your personal father. I want to hear you. Just ask Him to come into your life, save you from the sin in your life and come into your heart. Can you do that? Father, we're asking You, Lord, since this young man has come forward, we're asking You to save him today. We're asking You to come into his life, in Jesus' Mighty Name. We're asking You to save him, and cover him with the Blood of Jesus. Come into his life in Jesus' Mighty Name. Come into his life right now in the Name of Jesus. Let him be reassured today. Save him right now, Oh Jesus.

"We thank You, Jesus."

Magic With A Message

"We have a fear that somebody might get us wrong, that I can do magic because I'm gifted like Jesus. And it isn't that at all. I'm a magician, but the real magician is God. What I do is just tricks."
—Dock Haley

—The Fellowship of Christian Magicians was organized in San Francisco twenty years ago to provide an exchange for ideas and experiences among Christians who use magic for object lessons in Sunday schools and churches. It now has over twelve hundred members across the country. Its areas of interest have expanded to include a variety of media through which the Gospel message can be presented. These photos were taken at the Fellowship's annual conference.

"This year," President Ralph Mills told me, "we have twelve workshops scheduled in magic, twelve in ventriloquism, and twelve in chalk art and related visual fields. We have scheduled eleven training sessions in puppetry, five in gospel clowning, and two for balloon sculpturing."

Each of the workshops at the conference was designed to help members better prepare themselves for doing the Lord's work. The workshops included: "Presenting the Gospel with inexpensive magic equipment"; "How to keep ventriloquism appealing week after week in the local church"; "How to get started and incorporate chalk with preaching, Sunday school, Junior Church, and Special Ministries"; "How to reach children in the street and keep them interested (for gospel clowns)."

Evening programs featured performances in magic, ventriloquism, puppetry, a clown show and a talent contest for youngsters.

The annual conference of the Fellowship of Christian Magicians is held in Winona Lake, Indiana, at the Winona Lake Christian Assembly, home of "the World's Largest Bible Conference." About seven hundred "Christian Magicians" attended the week-long 1977 meeting.

One member, a postal worker from the state of Washington, told me that the trip cost him $750, some of which he had to borrow. "But it's worth it because of the encouragement I get here, and the willingness of everyone to share. Next year I plan to bring my wife with me."

"They call me America's number one gospel clown. But the thing is, I didn't do any of it, I didn't plan any of it, I didn't push it, I didn't promote it. God put things together. As you well see, I'm not prepared to be a clown—I didn't have the fancy clothes like the other clowns. When they all came out with this big title, I went and bought me a three hundred dollar clown suit. Man, that thing was gorgeous—now it's hanging in the closet. I'm comfortable in something like this.

"I was at the Clowns of America convention, and someone asked me where I do most of my shows. I said most are done in churches now. One guy said he gets lots of invitations, but he didn't know how to communicate in a church. So I shared with them what I do. And as I was coming home, I felt that there was a certain need for gospel clowns—for clowns to know how to apply the Gospel.

"I'm the founder of the Gospel Clowns of America. Our emblem is a clown holding an eternal light and an open Bible. It's not even a year old yet, and we have thirty-three paid members. I imagine by the time we get home we'll be in the neighborhood of a hundred because of the fact there were sixty or seventy people at the lecture here and they're all going to join. The only membership requirements are that you're saved and you're sharing.

"I'm the pastor of a little church in Brattleboro, Vermont, but this is my primary living. I'm training a lot of clowns. A lot of people are afraid to share their talent because they're afraid someone will put them out of business. But I don't see it that way. If I leave a church with a clown, I leave part of my ministry still there, working and going."

—Sparky The Clown

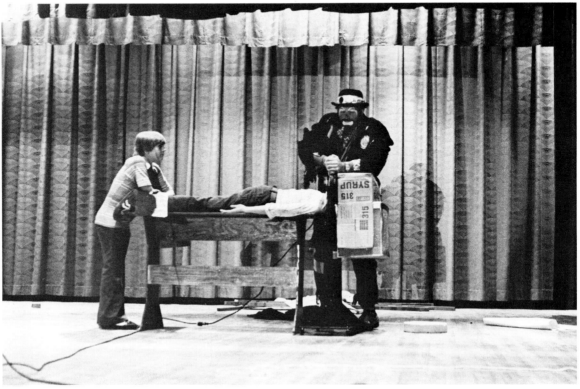

"It rained forty days and forty nights, and when they wanted to know how they could let the animals out of the Ark—remember what they did? They put a white handkerchief in a bag like this, and they sent out a dove. They sent out a dove, and he came back the first time—they sent another one and he came back with the olive branch. And the third time he stayed out.

"I'm sure you're all familiar with the dove from a silk that we use. My program ties together to the point that when I'm finished I have my two doves in here. The music starts again, and I vanish my two doves, and reappear two more. And that, basically, is what I do with Noah's Ark."

"Juggling is excellent visually. I found that when I did it at a church service, people were fascinated, almost hypnotized, by the balls going up and down. The interesting thing was, I had a young boy standing beside me feeding me the different colored balls as my story progressed. And what I would do is juggle two up in the air, and I'd put my hand out with the ball and he would replace it with the correct color, and I'd carry on. And the people's eyes were on the balls, and then all of a sudden there's another color. My wife was in the audience and people were asking her how I changed the color—they didn't realize that I was being fed. They were almost hypnotized.

"The message is very simple. I use the blue ball to represent God. In fact, I start out just by showing them the blue ball, and then I introduce the red ball, which is Jesus Christ. The color red reminds me of the Blood of Christ, and I just juggle the two. Then the white ball is introduced, which is God's Purity, the Holy Spirit. In the Bible there's the Trinity of God, and you're juggling the three of them at this time: you're juggling the three balls and you throw the blue one up higher and when you say God the Father, it falls down. Then you throw the red one up and say God the Son and you throw the white one up, it's sort of like an exclamation mark, it emphasizes what you're saying.

"So that's God the Father, God the Son, and God the Holy Spirit. You can do it maybe three times; it doesn't hurt to repeat it.

"Then you talk about the fellowship they had. God created heaven and the earth, as it's told in the Bible. God said it was good. And then God created man, and you introduce a pink ball, which represents man, and He said it was good. Then God created a helpmate for man, which was *very* good, and you introduce another pink ball. I do a change at that point and I've got a tri-colored ball which has got the blue, white, and red and I have the two pink balls. And we show then that they had fellowship, one with another, and they had a beautiful time in the Garden.

"Then I introduce the fact that they were disobedient to God. At this point I introduce a black one,

which represents sin. So you have the tri-color ball with the pink one and the black one, and you can do special trick juggling, where maybe God'll be here and man over here, still separated from God—there's all kinds of things you can do to emphasize what you're saying.

"Naturally when you're juggling, you have to keep your story lines very simple. You just say this! and this! and emphasizing it maybe with just a trick in between.

"I get rid of God all together at that point, and there's two black balls and man. And I talk about how man is constantly trying to reach God, and I throw it way up as high as I can. They never make it. Man always falls short of the glory of God. Why? Because we've sinned. And I stop at that point, and really very dramatically I say, 'Is that you?' Here's sin, and we cannot reach God, because we're disobedient.

"Then I say, but God loves us so very much that He didn't leave us here to deal with our own guilt and our own sin. In fact, He provided the way back, and I introduce the red ball again which is Christ, and I throw it way up and I say, Jesus Christ came down to earth to take away the sins of the world. He took upon His own self the punishment we deserved. And I go back to the juggling again, and I eliminate the black balls at that time and I introduce the Holy Spirit. Jesus said, when I go I will send another, the Holy Spirit, to come for you to lead you in all truth. And I end up with man, Jesus, and the Holy Spirit, these three.

"I'm a computer programmer. I've yet to use an illustration using a computer. Too complicated."

56

"I have specialized in paper tearing: that is, in the last ten years I've written ten books on paper tearing, consisting of a hundred lessons, each one different, no duplicates.

"I was in a terrible accident about eight or nine years ago. I had one leg cut off, and they sewed it back on because they didn't think I would live anyway. But after a year I was back on my feet, and during that time—I was in the hospital five months—I devised in my mind programs that would include paper tearing to illustrate a Gospel message. So in these last years I asked the Lord to let me live long enough to finish a hundred lessons which would make up ten books of ten chapters each.

"I have finished the tenth book now, so I'm waiting for the undertaker.

"I'm now going on eighty-one and I happen to be very active, except for this crippled leg.

"My special field has been visualization. My motto, or what I call a by-word on my publicity, is 'Visualize to Evangelize.' I tell the magicians I don't pull rabbits out of hats—I pull habits out of rats. My work has been primarily with young people and kids, and all these paper tearing lessons that I have usually wind up with an application of the Gospel. Many of the paper tears that I use wind up with the tearing out of a cross, because that's basic to anybody's experience with God.

"The hourglass—just take a piece of paper and fold it twice and make two tears, and you have an hourglass, and then fold it again and make a cross out of it. I call that 'Time marches on.' That's the kind of thing I do.

"I tell about how the hourglass was invented so many hundreds of years ago in Alexandria, Egypt. Then a few hundred years later it was part of the pulpit furniture, and the pastor was governed by the sand in the hourglass—when it ran out, he was supposed to stop. And I say it was better than the cough drop method, when one preacher put a cough drop in his mouth, and when it was gone, he quit preaching. By mistake one day, he got a button in his mouth, and the message was both tasteless and endless.

"I put a lot of humor in it to make it interesting to the kids."

—Arnold Carl Westphal

"I carry in my wallet four blank cards. It's a great way to sit down and talk with somebody. 'Sir, have you seen this?' People admittedly want to see what you've got. You show four blank cards; you lay them down and you have them choose cards and you end up with one card. When they turn it over, it has a picture of Christ or the word Jesus on it. And you can go into patter about accepting the Lord—God gives us a choice and either we accept Him or we don't. I like doing card tricks in that vein."

"The idea about Captain Hook came while I was in college. I had lost an arm and a leg in a motorcycle accident in 1960, riding with a rough motorcycle crowd. I woke up in the hospital after two days of unconsciousness and my mother explained to me what had happened. I just really couldn't believe that it had happened to me. She shared with me that the only way my life could be saved was to have my arm and leg amputated because they were so badly crushed and mangled. So there in the hospital it seemed like the end of the world for me, no hope, the sky was so dark and grey. It was there that I became a Christian, and accepted Christ as my savior. My whole life made an about face from that moment, when I accepted Him. I had to learn to walk again, learn to wash my elbow with one hand, learn to do a lot of things. But I found out if you want to do something bad enough, you can do it, if God is on your side.

"I began to walk again, and began to attend church regularly. I felt the Lord speak to my heart about going to college to finish my education. So I went, and it was there that I felt the calling to the ministry, and I met my wife, Mrs. Hook.

"Our last name is Saum, pronounced like the book in the Bible, except spelled differently. We were married, and it was then that the idea came to dress up like Captain Hook.

"After graduating from Southern Bible College in Houston, I was associate pastor of a church and I

shared with the pastor this idea that I had. He just went wild about it, so we tried it for a weekend. It was such a success that he and I both agreed that this was God's will, to go out and minister to kids across the nation. So in thirty days we started traveling all over the United States, telling an old story a new way—the Gospel story, pirate-style.

"I'm a ventriloquist, and we have a television show that goes into about two hundred outlets in cities across the United States and four or five foreign countries. It's called 'Pirate Adventures with Captain Hook and his Crew.' It's just all coming together. So the Lord's blessing our program.

"My disability's become my ability. The stumbling stone that was thrown my way has become a stepping stone for me, and I plan to take a million boys and girls through the portals of heaven to present to the Lord Jesus Christ.

"Someone says, 'Captain, how many were saved at your last meeting?' Well, every week that varies, but I'll say, for instance, a hundred and fifty and a half. They'll say, 'A hundred and fifty and a half? What do you mean?' Well, a hundred and fifty boys and girls received Christ, and one adult: when you save a little child from a life of sin and corruption, you've captured his entire life, but when you save an adult, they just have a little bit left, so that was the half.

"God's really blessing our ministry. We travel over a hundred thousand miles a year. We have several different long play albums out, we have three song books and a coloring book. We have an artist working right now on a Captain Hook comic book, like the ones of Corrie Ten Boom or Johnny Cash. So we're really excited about all the things that are happening. A company just called me the other day to talk about a Captain Hook game.

"But all of these things carry a message. If it doesn't testify of Christ, or lift up Christ, there's no sense for me to be involved, because God's called me to minister and to preach, and He's helping me to do it.

"The devil would like to get me off someplace somewhere else, because he doesn't want me telling boys and girls about the Lord. But this is my whole life, and this is the whole thing that I live for. You can beat the devil all over with the Lord's Book. You can just say, 'Hey devil, you're a liar,' and run him out of your path."

—Captain Hook

Singing, Shouting, Preaching, Praying

"I made a statement last night in Jackson, Mississippi, and I want to make the same statement here tonight. Did you notice the line in the song? It just struck me last night. I know you've sung the song a hundred times, maybe a thousand times: 'The Old Rugged Cross, the emblem of suffering and shame.' 'The emblem,' signifying that this is the product. You walk up to a Coke machine and you put in that quarter and out comes Coca-Cola. The emblem across the Coca-Cola signifies 'the real thing.' Let me tell you something. The emblem of suffering and shame is the cross that Jesus died on. It signifies that it is the true product, the real thing. I want you to know, when you stand for a song like that, I don't want you to stand for me. I don't want you to praise me. But if you stand for the *emblem,* the Old Rugged Cross, Hallelujah, that's all right."

—The Happy Goodman Family

—It takes eight hours to drive from Greenville to Waycross in south Georgia. It's almost all on interstate highway, so there's not much more to do than listen to the local radio stations and get into the mood. This is the first real all-night sing I've been to. The others, urban all-weather adaptations, were indoors, never actually lasting the entire night—and auditoriums can be pretty uncomfortable over the long haul.

I get to the stadium early enough to park near the gate, find the head man of the local Shriners who have sponsored the sing, and have the back of my hand stamped so I can leave and get back in. The Happy Goodmans, the Tennesseans and the Sego Brothers pull their buses onto the field close to the stage. They hang around, talking with friends in other groups, with fans and with Shriners out on the field, while their road crews unload steel guitars, drums, basses and amps, and carry racks and boxes of records up to the concession area inside the stadium.

The program begins with the amateur talent contest: each group has four minutes in which to do one song, with absolutely no talking. They'll be graded on personal appearance, musical ability and stage presence by judges who are professional gospel singers or promoters.

The crowd comes in waves, carrying the things they'll need to make it through the night: food and drinks, lawn chairs, blankets and pillows, jackets and sweaters, waterproof plastic sheeting, books, cards, games. Kids play, chase dogs around the field, nag at parents. The largest part of the audience won't get here until after work, but those who come early can stake out the area they want and have plenty to do.

The talent contest ends around dinner time; the winner of the recording contract is announced after the dinner break. Before the show each of the groups makes its sales pitch for records, song books, picture albums, fancy Bibles—all at special-for-the-sing prices. Most of them are still dressed for traveling; they'll change just before their first show.

I've seen most of the performers before, and I know which ones will just sing, which ones will do a little testifying, and which ones will get down and preach. They all go around once and then start again—the bigger name groups go on earlier during the second show, and they leave soon after.

By midnight, the people start to leave. Those who plan to stay until the end catch naps. A few leave, go home or to the motel, and then come back. By 4 A.M., though, it seems to be a mutual decision between the entertainers and the audience to call things to an end. The last remaining buses are loaded up and pull out. The last few fans leave slowly. This is the ultimate gospel concert: a lot of music and plenty of entertainment for the money.

"Remember, these people are here to break into this business and to do more for their Savior and to try to get involved more deeply in gospel music; so they're here to do their best for you."

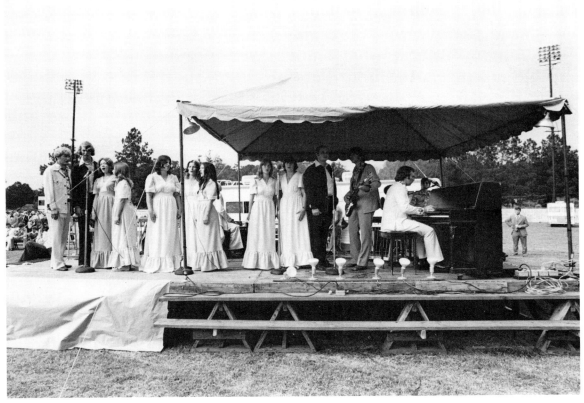

73

"Reach out and touch Jesus. See the most beautiful part of God. The most precious part of Glory is that He loves you as much as He loves me, or me as much as He loves you. He's no respecter of persons. And the same God came in one instant, just in the midst of while I was sitting in the lobby, waiting to be checked in at the Mayo Clinic, in Rochester, Minnesota. I sat there in a wheelchair and Howard registered me in to be there for no-telling how long, to go through tests for a heart problem. The doctors said there was no cure, that I must learn to live with pain. I must learn to never get excited, or get in a crowd, or do anything that would exert me.

"But Oh, sweet Jesus, one touch from Him took it all away. Just one touch from Him and it was all washed away. Praise God, Hallelujah! Dear God, I got an urge to run!

"I stayed in that hospital in Rochester, Minnesota, the famous Mayo Clinic, for a whole week and went through all kinds of tests, only for them to discover that what I had been telling them since the day I walked in there had really happened: God had performed a miracle. They can't find no heart disease. The handful of medicine that I carry in a kit that I got to keep handy at all times, they said you don't need them no more—do anything you want to.

"I tell these boys, and I scare them to death. Rusty told you I couldn't climb no steps—the doctor said don't ever climb steps again. And when I get to steps now I run up 'em, just to get even with the devil.

"Some of the greatest people in the world are the physicians of our land. And I'm smart enough to know that. They're so wonderful, and they're so intelligent, and they've learned so much, and they're so kind and considerate. And their knowledge is so fantastic, until they went in my heart, replaced arteries, and fixed it.

"But I still got a heart disease that they can't fix. But I was acquainted with One that knew how to master all of it. And the very instant that He said now it's time, I felt heaven when it opened up. And now if you can find faith, reach out. You that got a need, reach out and touch Jesus."

—Sister Vestal Goodman

"Really, you don't see too much outdoor, big singing like this. I watched and listened to the Sego Brothers and Naomi sing a while ago. James talked about—he always talks about—when he was an alcoholic, how God came down when he was at his lowest, in '41. I saw the Happy Goodman singers come on. I saw The Kingsmen sing. I heard Squire testify to you. I heard Sister Vestal tell you how God, just at her lowest, reached and picked her up and healed her in a marvelous way.

"I was walking back out through here as she was talking and singing, and I was remembering what James said, how God took the alcohol from him. And I thought, what has God really done for me? I never was an alcoholic, I've never been marvelously healed from any dread disease. What has God really done for me? And I got one of the best blessings I guess I've got in a long time, right out there in the middle of the football field.

"He said, I saved you from a burning hell. If you don't have any other testimony than that, brother, I think you've got a winner.

"I'm glad that when God saved me He put something deep down inside.

"No, I never was a drug addict. No, I never was an alcoholic. No, God never did really touch my body and heal me. But He saved me. He saved me from something worse than alcohol. He healed me from something mighty worse than a heart attack. He saved me and He healed me from my sins. Boy, and I'll tell you what: I feel something running up and down my arms, burning up, my sweat pouring off me, and goose bumps running all over me.

"I'm glad that when God looked down and saw that young man that night, looking up, calling upon His Name to forgive him, save him from his sins, I'm glad He had mercy on me.

"Boy, I'd like to hear somebody say Amen real loud right now.

"This may be outside, and it's supposed to be a singing, you're just supposed to come and eat pop-corn and hot dogs and have a good time. But I'm glad there's still some places you can come and have a gospel sing and still feel something moving in your soul.

"And I'll have to say, the first three groups that I heard tonight, they had that for you. They presented the Gospel to you, and I'm glad that the Tennesseans can stand here before you tonight and say that if I can't say nothing else, that I know Jesus Christ is my Savior, and I know that one of these days when He splits that Eastern sky, He's coming after me. Whew! I feel something. I'm glad that when God saved me He didn't give me the type of religion where I sit down on Sunday morning and listen to some little Doctor Popsicle give me a little sermonette. I'm glad that when God saved me He gave me something I can feel."

—Willie Wynn

Get Ready For Your Miracle

"Well, here we are, in another Greenville service. Just think: some of you that are blind, you'll go away seeing; some of you that are deaf, they'll go away hearing; those that were dumb, go away speaking. And you that came in crippled, how wonderful to go out walking. It's marvelous, marvelous indeed, what the Lord is doing with His fantastic miracles. The annointing is getting greater and greater every week through this ministry. It's totally unreal, this sixth sense called the Faith sense, that it's really happening. It is being done. It's just what God promised."

—Reverend Ernest Angley

—Services at Reverend Ernest Angley's Grace Cathedral in Akron, Ohio, are held on Friday nights. The rest of the time the Ernest Angley Miracle Crusade is on the road. This weekend they're in Greenville, South Carolina.

Having failed to reach Angley at his home base, I go to the Greenville Memorial Auditorium. There I find the Ernest Angley Miracle Hour video truck parked alongside two private buses, and the Angley team—a gospel quartet, musicians, assistants, ushers, a sound engineer and the TV crew. They are friendly, but firm: I cannot photograph or record during the service without Angley's permission. I might be able to speak with "the Rev" briefly before the service starts, but only if he has the time.

Angley arrives by car from a nearby motel, and we talk backstage. He expresses interest in my project, and agrees to let me work as long as I "don't interfere with the workings of the Holy Spirit." While we talk, Angley seems to be looking more closely at my assistant than at me. Later, she tells me that she felt he could actually see the "black border, about half an inch wide" around her lips, signifying her possession by the "nicotine demon," an evil spirit which Angley describes in his newsletter, *The Power of the Holy Ghost.*

Showtime. People with every imaginable physical and mental affliction fill the auditorium, coming to receive a "miracle cure." These are not merely the confirmed Christians I have seen at revivals and the like; they are believers, in need and with hope. They come in wheelchairs, or using walkers, canes, crutches. Parents carry sick infants and disabled children. The non-ambulatory and more severely physically handicapped are escorted to an "invalids only" section. I am not prepared for this: to me, the hope seems more like desperation.

I talk to people—a woman with a supposedly incurable heart defect until Angley touched her; a man whose leg had been crippled in a trucking accident, then made normal again; a friend who tells me that Angley cured him of a painful stomach condition which had defeated the doctors. I listen to testimonies from people who come to the stage, incredible stories of healing and miracles that occurred at services in the past.

I stay for more than eight hours on Saturday, and return for the Sunday service. It is more of the same: cripples walk away carrying their crutches; blind people who have to be escorted to the stage tell Angley how many fingers he holds in front of them; deaf and dumb children, in strained voices, answer Angley's questions and repeat the words he says to them.

It is the expression on these people's faces that bears witness to Angley's claims of miracles. Never again do I see the intensity of true belief that is present here.

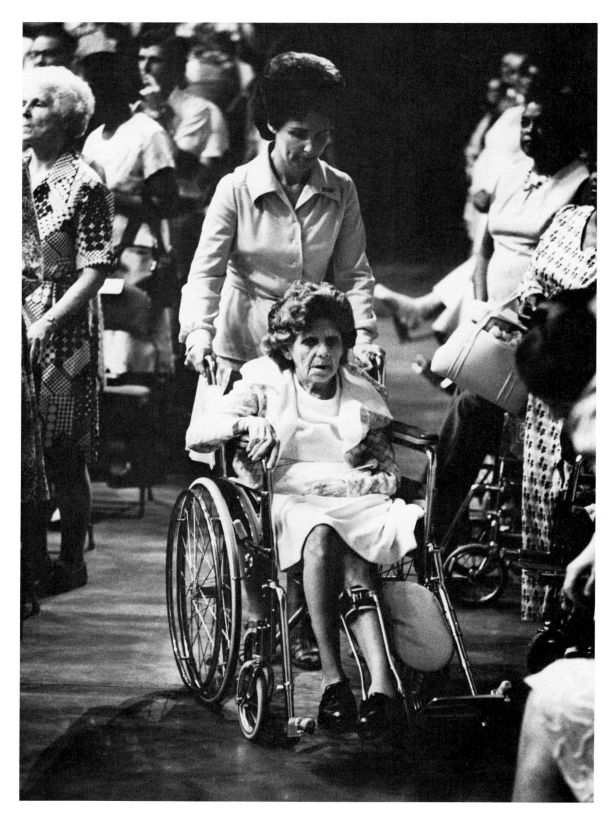

"You that have come for a miracle . . . get ready for that miracle. Get ready. You say, 'How, preacher?' By yielding to the Holy Spirit, and letting the Holy Spirit condition you for your miracle. He'll get you ready. Just lend an ear to Him. Let Him turn the Word of God over in your mind. And He'll take the Word, the sword, and cut out all the doubt, all the fear, all the frustration. It'll be so easy for you to reach out and touch Jesus.

"It's all right to go to a doctor if you can cast his opinion down where it belongs, and when God says I am the Lord that healeth thee, you take what God says in preference to what the physician says, because your physician is only human. I appreciate your doctors and hospitals, and we're reaching into the medical people. They're coming to the miracle services at Grace Cathedral. There's a doctor right there to watch the miracle services each Friday night. His practice is right there in Akron. He brings and sends patients in that's been healed by the power of God."

95

"This is healing from Heaven. All cancer victims—the doctor has said cancer—come to the platform. The doctor has said cancer—come quickly. . . . You that are cancer victims, if you're not in the invalid section, come quickly. The doctor said cancer: you didn't think it up, you didn't dream it up: the *doctor* said cancer. Come to the platform. Thousands, literally thousands, have been healed of cancer through this ministry. All cancer victims, come on. Remember, no more cancer. In just a moment it's all over. Thank God. Yeah, thou cancer spirits, COME OUT! No more cancer. Thank God. Are you saved? No more cancer. And oh God, re-create those parts that have been destroyed. Oh, if we only had count of all that's been healed of cancer, it would be a staggering figure. Any more cancer victims? This is healing from Heaven."

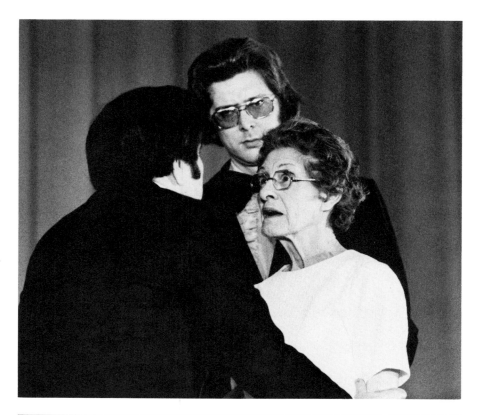

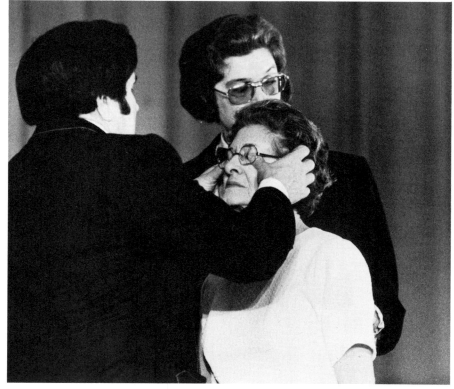

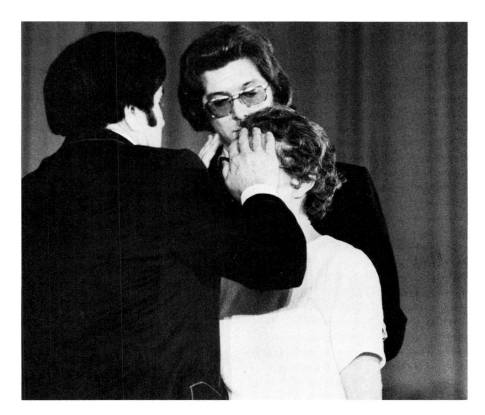

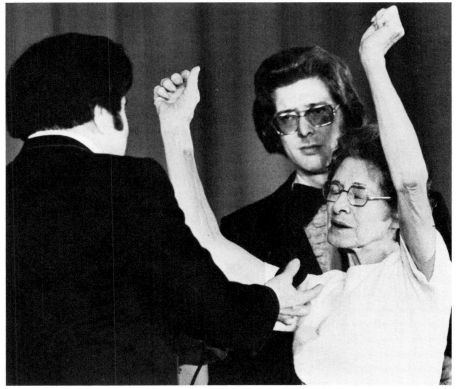

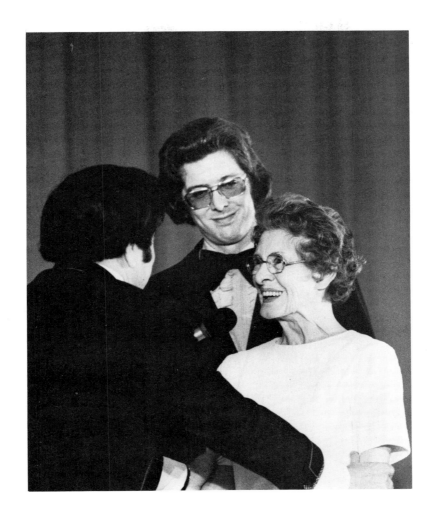

—The lady's Baptist; she has a cataract on the right eye, and hardening of the arteries.

"Here goes. You know that, don't you? In the Name of Jesus, thou old foul spirit called cataract—
OUT! Open that eye and look right at the man of God. Look here. You see me good? It's done. I'm glad.
They just vanish with the power of God."

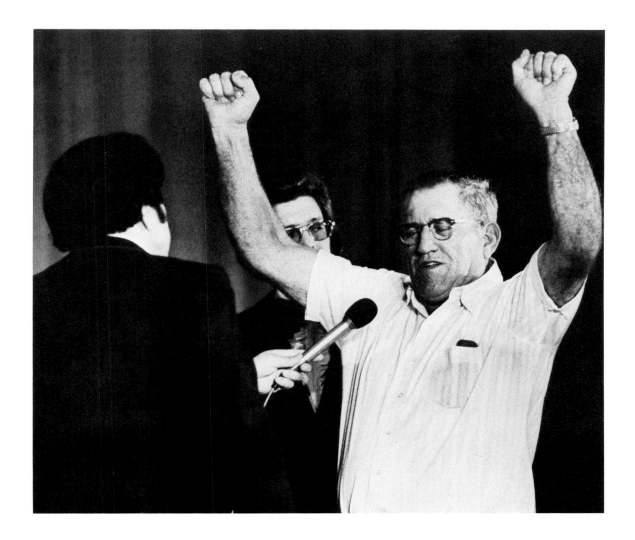

—The gentleman is from the Church of God, has a roaring in the right ear, is hard of hearing with nerve deafness in both ears, and he has a hernia.

"He has two hearing aids. He has them out now. In the Name of Jesus, thank the Lord: I know You would do it. Foul deaf spirits, in the Name of Jesus, come out—OUT! Amen. Praise the Lord. I can hear.
—I can hear.

"I don't need a hearing aid."
—I don't need a hearing aid.

"I am healed."
—I am healed.

"Hold up your hearing aids. You've got two of them. Hold them up. You've got a roaring. Let's get rid of that. I command it to never roar again!"

"To my right, in the balcony, there's an arthritic condition being healed. It is a lady; stand to your feet and rejoice, dear lady over there. Arthritis! Come and stand up over there, in the balcony. Hurry, you're being healed. Stand up, lift up both hands, and declare your miracle. Declare your miracle! Amen. It happened, didn't it? Yes, yes, yes!"

"When blind spirits leave a person, that person can see. I place my fingers in deaf ears and command those spirits to come out in the Name of Jesus; God has given me power over demon spirits."
—Ernest Angley in THE POWER OF THE HOLY GHOST

"God made man. God made woman. And He knows how to repair man and woman, doesn't He?"

Come As You Are

For where two or three are gathered in my name, there am I in the midst of them.

—Matthew 18:20

To K.C. For J.C.

Dear Member of the Press:

On July 20-24, from 60,000 to 100,000 Christians from across the United States will gather in Kansas City, Missouri, for the 1977 Conference on Charismatic Renewal in the Christian Churches. Because of the recent rapid growth of the Charismatic movement, the interdenominational nature of the event, and the large number of participants, it is already being hailed by many as the most significant religious event of this century.

—Ronn Kerr, announcement, Conference Press Public Relations Service

—The 1977 Conference on Charismatic Renewal in the Christian Churches is the largest ecumenically-sponsored gathering in history, according to conference sources. More than 50,000 Christians of every major denomination have come here to Kansas City for a five-day series of seminars, workshops and programs covering the full range of the charismatic experience. The conference reflects the fastest growing grassroots religious movement in the country.

Traditionally, charismatic means being graced by God to function as a member of the Body of Christ. The word is now used to designate a movement within the church, and the people who are identified with it. Charismatics believe that the Holy Spirit is once again showering his gifts and graces on the earth, and renewing the churches and the lives of individual Christians. The result is a freer, more spontaneous, more exciting and more involved form of religious expression and worship. It has put new life back into the church.

The key element in the movement is baptism in the Holy Spirit, which takes place in the context of intense prayer and the laying-on of hands by Spirit-filled Christians. Most charismatics believe that the definitive evidence of this baptism is the gift of speaking in tongues, described as a "form of non-discursive, spontaneous prayer—a verbal expression independent of any specific linguistic structure."

At the conference individual denominational meetings are held during the day at sites scattered throughout the city. Then everyone returns to Arrowhead Stadium, home of the Kansas City Chiefs, for the evening programs, which feature speeches by well-known religious leaders, pep talks and instruction on being charismatic, and prayers and singing. All major religious and secular publications, newspapers and broadcast media are here, and the conference is reported to have received the most extensive press coverage of any religious event.

"The theme of the conference is 'Jesus is Lord.' Our theme is simple, yet extremely profound. In the oneness which we are experiencing, we want to grow in our understanding of His Lordship. We want to receive from Him wholeness and holiness. We seek to be equipped with gifts, graces, tools and weapons which we need to build up and strengthen the Christian community today and to proclaim the Gospel in an effective way in contemporary society.

"We believe that the conference will be used by the Lord to advance the goal of His prayer for Christian unity, that it will be a spiritual threshold which we will cross together into a new era of being one in the Spirit.

"What is more significant than the total number of people attending is the fact of the diverse church bodies from which the conference participants are coming. This is a conference of brothers and sisters in Christ who are normally separated from each other. We are coming together in unity around the Lordship of Jesus Christ and in the power of the Holy Spirit to worship the Father and to give common witness to the life we share."

—Kevin M. Ranaghan, Chairman of CCRCC Planning Committee

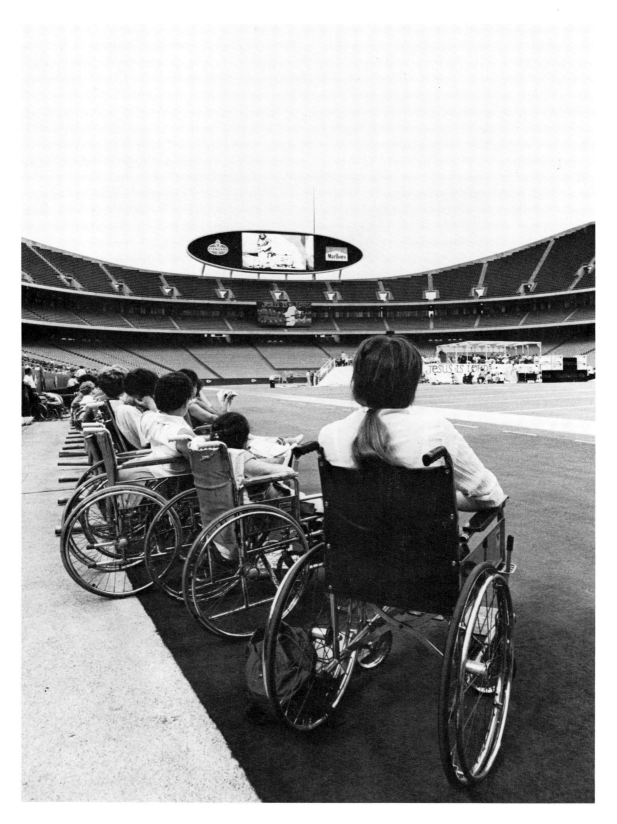

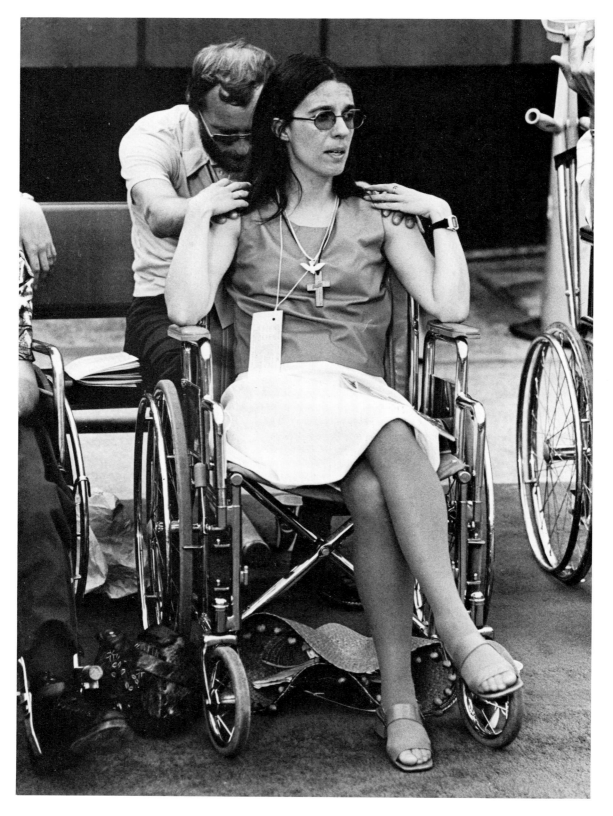

"It's like a BEFORE and AFTER picture in Kansas City—before the 1977 CCRCC, and after your arrival. You should all know that you have made a difference. More accurately, of course, Jesus Christ is making a difference through you. The difference is a subtle, and yet quite discernible peace which has settled on the downtown area since Wednesday. That peace can be seen in people's faces. Smiles radiate the joy of His presence. Hustle and bustle of a hurried people in a central business district have given way noticeably to a more leisurely—and more meaningful— more thoughtful pace.

"Complaints to harrassed waitresses and cashiers are giving way to compassion for their immediate discomfort. Restlessness of long lines is giving way to gentle and smiling conversations. Driving habits have settled into a 'speed-limit-or-below' routine in place of the Rat Race. Drivers who must change lanes are being afforded plenty of room and a courteous go-ahead. Cleanliness abounds, with scraps properly disposed of by the throngs. The words 'Thank you' are music to calloused ears.

"Above all is the deep sincerity. It is not the result of obedience to law, or a desire to be recognized for recognition's sake. It is genuine love. The Love of Jesus. It is not pretense. It is real.

"And your actions are having their effect on my city. My town will not be the same when you leave. Because when you go back, to your homes, you will have left a part of yourselves here. You will have stamped the presence of God clearly on this city."

—A letter from a Kansas City native in the CCRCC Newsletter